SCHOLASTIC

W9-DCA-734

Word Family Trees

New York · Toronto · London · Auckland · Sydney
Mexico City · New Delhi · Hong Kong · Buenos Aires

Teaching *Resources*

Edited by Immacula A. Rhodes

Cover design by Jason Robinson

Interior design by Sydney Wright

ISBN: 978-0-545-30069-8

3 4 5 6 7 8 9 10   40   18 17 16 15 14 13 12 11

Contents

Word Family Trees

Short Vowels

Long Vowels

Variant Vowels

Introduction

Word Family Trees offers an engaging and fun way for kids to master more than 50 different word families. Research shows that learning to recognize and becoming familiar with word family patterns is an important component in building reading confidence and fluency. Repeated encounters with word families and their spelling patterns helps children more easily and automatically decode other words that contain the same patterns. This "automaticity" helps lay the foundation for long-term reading success.

The activities in this book give children lots of practice in reading and writing words in the same word family. As children complete the words on the apples, they further develop phonemic awareness skills by determining which beginning letters or letter combinations work with the word family ending to create actual words. And the repeated exposure to word family spelling patterns helps boost children's spelling skills.

You can use the word family trees with the whole class or in small groups. Or place them in a learning center for children to use independently or in pairs. The activities are ideal for children of all learning styles, ELL students, and for RTI instruction. And best of all, the word family trees take only a few minutes to complete, making them a quick way to integrate word family instruction into your school day.

Connections to the Language Arts Standards

The activities in this book are designed to support you in meeting the following standards for students in grades K–2 as outlined by Mid-continent Research for Education and Learning (McREL), an organization that collects and synthesizes national and state K–12 curriculum standards.

Reading

- Uses basic elements of phonetic analysis (letter/sound relationships, beginning consonants, vowel sounds, blends, and word patterns) to decode unknown words
- Uses basic elements of structural analysis, such as spelling patterns, to decode unknown words

Writing

- Uses phonics knowledge and conventions of spelling in writing (uses letter/sound relationships and spells basic short-vowel, long-vowel, r-controlled, and consonant-blend patterns)

Source: Kendall, J. S. and Marzano, R. J. (2004). *Content knowledge: A compendium of standards and benchmarks for K–12 education.* Aurora, CO: Mid-continent Research for Education and Learning. Online database: http://www.mcrel.org/standards-benchmarks/

How to Use the Word Family Trees

Completing a word family tree is easy and fun. To begin, distribute copies of the activity page for the word family you want to teach. Point out the word family ending on the basket that's under the tree and name it. Then have children do the following:

1. Look at the letter and letter combinations on the tree trunk. Sound out each one in front of the word family ending to see if it makes an actual word.

2. If the letter(s) make a word, write it on an apple to spell out that word.

3. After filling in all the apples, read the words aloud, pointing to each word while saying it.

Check pages 6–8 for a list of words that can be created for each word family tree.

Activities to Extend Learning

Use these activities to give children additional opportunities to explore word families.

Make Your Own Tree: Use the word family template on page 64 to create your own word family trees. Simply label a copy of the tree with the word family of your choice. Copy and distribute the page. Then have children write words that belong to the word family on the apples. You might also give copies of the template to children so they can make their own word family trees.

Alphabetical Apples: Write words that belong to a word family on red apple cutouts (one word per apple). Put the cutouts in a learning center. Invite children to put the words in alphabetical order. When finished, challenge them to read the words in sequence as quickly as possible.

Shape Books: For shape books, mask the apples on a copy of the tree template (page 64) and make colored copies of it on sturdy paper. Also, cut a class supply of plain paper into quarters. To make a book, have children cut out the tree, then stack and staple 6–8 pages to the treetop. Ask them to choose a word family (or assign a word family to children) and write it on the top page. Have children write one word that belongs to their word family on each of the remaining pages and then illustrate those words. Invite children to read their mini-books with partners.

Word Family Memory: To make game cards for this familiar game, simply write word family words on a supply of apple cutouts (one word per card). Check that each word belongs to a pair. Then invite children to use the cards to play Memory. Each time children find a pair of words that belong to the same word family, they keep the match.

Musical Word Walk: Label sheets of paper with words from several different word families, checking that each word belongs to a pair. Arrange the pages word-side down in a looped path. Then have children walk along the outside of the path while music plays. Periodically stop the music, have children pick up the nearest page, and then find another child with a word that belongs to the same word family.

Word Detectives: Assign word family endings to individuals or pairs. Then ask children to search the room for objects and words that belong to their word family. Have them write their findings on paper to share with the class.

Word Families on the Move: Call out action words that belong to different word families. For instance, you might call out *jump, run, throw, hop, slide, swim, clap,* or *stand.* After saying each word, have children perform the action. Then ask them to name other words belonging to the same word family.

Word Family Word Lists

-ack (page 9)
back
pack
rack
sack
tack
black
crack
quack
shack
snack
stack
track

-an (page 10)
ban
can
fan
man
pan
ran
tan
van
bran
plan
scan
than

-ank (page 11)
bank
lank
rank
sank
tank
yank
blank
clank
crank
drank
plank
thank

-ap (page 12)
cap
lap
map
nap
rap
tap
clap
flap
snap
trap
scrap
wrap

-ash (page 13)
bash
cash
dash
hash
mash
rash
clash
flash
slash
smash
stash
trash

-at (page 14)
bat
cat
fat
hat
mat
pat
rat
sat
brat
chat
flat
that

-ed (page 15)
bed
fed
led
red
wed
bled
bred
fled
shed
sled
sped
shred

-ell (page 16)
bell
cell
dell
fell
sell
tell
well
yell
shell
smell
spell
swell

-en (page 17)
Ben
den
hen
Jen
men
pen
ten
yen
Glen
then
when
wren

-ent (page 18)
bent
cent
dent
gent
lent
rent
sent
tent
vent
went
scent
spent

-est (page 19)
best
jest
nest
pest
rest
test
vest
west
zest
chest
crest
quest

-ick (page 20)
kick
lick
pick
sick
wick
brick
chick
flick
quick
stick
thick
trick

-ill (page 21)
bill
fill
hill
pill
will
chill
grill
quill
skill
spill
twill
thrill

-in (page 22)
fin
kin
pin
tin
win
chin
grin
shin
skin
spin
thin
twin

-ing (page 23)
ding
king
ring
sing
wing
zing
fling
swing
thing
spring
string
wring

-ink (page 24)
link
mink
pink
rink
sink
wink
blink
clink
drink
stink
think
shrink

-ip (page 25)
dip
rip
tip
zip
chip
flip
grip
ship
skip
snip
whip
strip

-it (page 26)
bit
fit
hit
lit
pit
sit
wit
grit
quit
skit
split
knit

-ob (page 27)
cob
job
lob
mob
rob
sob
blob
glob
slob
snob
throb
knob

-ock (page 28)
dock
lock
mock
rock
sock
block
crock
flock
frock
shock
stock
knock

Word Family Word Lists

(continued)

-og *(page 29)*	-uck *(page 33)*	-ail *(page 37)*	-ame *(page 41)*	-ee *(page 45)*
bog	buck	bail	came	bee
cog	duck	fail	dame	fee
dog	luck	jail	fame	see
fog	muck	mail	game	tee
hog	puck	pail	lame	wee
jog	suck	sail	name	flee
log	tuck	tail	same	free
clog	cluck	wail	tame	glee
flog	pluck	flail	blame	tree
frog	stuck	quail	flame	spree
slog	truck	snail	frame	three
smog	struck	trail	shame	knee

-op *(page 30)*	-ug *(page 34)*	-ain *(page 38)*	-ate *(page 42)*	-eed *(page 46)*
cop	bug	gain	date	deed
hop	dug	main	fate	feed
mop	hug	pain	gate	heed
pop	jug	rain	hate	need
top	mug	vain	late	reed
chop	rug	brain	mate	seed
crop	tug	chain	rate	weed
drop	chug	drain	crate	bleed
flop	plug	grain	grate	freed
plop	smug	plain	plate	greed
prop	snug	stain	skate	speed
shop	shrug	sprain	state	tweed

-ot *(page 31)*	-ump *(page 35)*	-ake *(page 39)*	-ay *(page 43)*	-eep *(page 47)*
cot	bump	bake	bay	beep
got	dump	cake	day	deep
hot	hump	make	hay	jeep
jot	jump	rake	jay	keep
not	lump	sake	lay	peep
pot	pump	wake	may	weep
rot	clump	brake	way	cheep
blot	grump	flake	gray	creep
shot	plump	quake	play	sheep
spot	stump	shake	stay	sleep
trot	thump	snake	tray	steep
knot	trump	stake	spray	sweep

-ub *(page 32)*	-unk *(page 36)*	-ale *(page 40)*	-eat *(page 44)*	-ice *(page 48)*
cub	bunk	bale	beat	dice
hub	dunk	gale	heat	lice
nub	hunk	hale	meat	mice
rub	junk	male	neat	nice
sub	sunk	pale	peat	rice
tub	chunk	sale	seat	vice
club	drunk	tale	bleat	price
grub	flunk	vale	cheat	slice
snub	skunk	scale	cleat	spice
stub	spunk	shale	pleat	thrice
scrub	trunk	stale	treat	twice
shrub	shrunk	whale	wheat	

7

Word Family Word Lists

(continued)

-ide *(page 49)*
hide
ride
side
tide
wide
bride
chide
glide
pride
slide
snide
stride

-ight *(page 50)*
fight
light
might
night
right
sight
tight
bright
flight
fright
plight
knight

-ine *(page 51)*
dine
fine
line
mine
nine
pine
vine
shine
spine
swine
whine
shrine

-y *(page 52)*
by
my
cry
dry
fly
fry
pry
shy
sky
spy
try
why

-oke *(page 53)*
coke
joke
poke
woke
yoke
broke
choke
smoke
spoke
stoke
stroke

-one *(page 54)*
bone
cone
hone
lone
tone
zone
clone
drone
phone
prone
shone
stone

-ow *(page 55)*
bow
low
mow
row
tow
blow
crow
glow
grow
show
snow
know

-all *(page 56)*
ball
call
fall
gall
hall
mall
tall
wall
small
stall
squall

-ar *(page 57)*
bar
car
far
jar
mar
par
tar
char
scar
spar
star

-are *(page 58)*
bare
care
dare
fare
mare
rare
ware
glare
share
spare
stare
square

-ark *(page 59)*
bark
dark
hark
lark
mark
park
Clark
shark
spark
stark

-aw *(page 60)*
caw
jaw
law
paw
raw
saw
claw
draw
flaw
slaw
thaw
straw

-ore *(page 61)*
bore
core
more
pore
sore
tore
wore
chore
score
shore
snore
store

-oop *(page 62)*
coop
hoop
loop
droop
scoop
sloop
snoop
stoop
swoop
troop

-out *(page 63)*
bout
gout
pout
rout
clout
scout
shout
snout
spout
stout
trout
sprout

Name: _____ Date: _____

__ack   __ack

__ack   __ack

__ack

__ack   __ack

__ack

__ack   __ack

__ack   __ack

bl	ch	p	r
v	st	tr	sn
b	f	sh	qu
k	cr	s	t

-ack

Name: _____ Date: _____

___an   ___an

___an   ___an

___an   ___an

___an   ___an

___an   ___an

___an   ___an

gl	g	w	pl
b	m	sc	p
c	br	t	th
f	r	dr	v

-an

b   cr   r   tr

bl   l   pl   z

g   dr   s   y

cl   m   t   th

-ank

Name: _____ Date: _____

___ap
___ap
___ap
___ap
___ap
___ap
___ap
___ap
___ap
___ap
___ap
___ap

br	f	sh	t
c	scr	m	wr
cl	l	sn	r
d	fl	n	tr

-ap

fr   d   fl   h

b   cl   m   st

sn   f   r   t

c   sl   sm   tr

-ash

Name: _____   Date: _____

____at   ____at

____at   ____at

____at   ____at

____at   ____at

____at   ____at

____at   ____at

b	j	g	r
c	fl	m	sn
ch	h	th	s
f	k	p	br

-at

Name: _____ Date: _____

____ed   ____ed

____ed   ____ed

____ed   ____ed

____ed   ____ed

____ed   ____ed

____ed   ____ed

bl	g	shr	sp
b	br	k	w
fl	l	sl	y
f	sh	r	th

-ed

Name: _____ Date: _____

____ell ____ell

____ell ____ell ____ell

____ell ____ell ____ell

____ell ____ell ____ell

____ell ____ell ____ell

sn	f	sm	w
b	k	s	y
c	sh	t	sw
d	m	sp	tr

-ell

Name: _____   Date: _____

___en

___en

___en

___en

___en

___en

___en

___en

___en

___en

___en

___en

___en

B	sc	m	wr
cr	J	wh	v
d	l	p	y
h	th	t	Gl

-en

Name: _____ Date: _____

_____ent
_____ent
_____ent
_____ent
_____ent
_____ent
_____ent
_____ent
_____ent
_____ent
_____ent
_____ent

b	g	fr	t
sc	h	m	v
c	gl	r	w
d	l	s	sp

-ent

Name: _____   Date: _____

___est

___est

___est

___est

___est

___est

___est

___est

___est

___est

___est

___est

w	n	cr	b
ch	p	s	z
j	r	t	qu
k	pl	v	tr

-est

Name: _____ Date: _____

___ick ___ick

___ick ___ick

___ick

___ick ___ick

___ick ___ick

___ick

___ick ___ick

br	j	qu	s
b	fl	l	th
ch	k	st	w
g	gr	p	tr

-ick

Name: _____   Date: _____

b   qu   n   thr
ch   h   sn   v
f   sk   p   tw
gr   l   sp   w

-ill

Name: _____ Date: _____

___in
___in
___in
___in
___in
___in
___in
___in
___in
___in
___in
___in

ch	k	sl	t
f	sh	p	th
gr	n	sp	w
j	sk	r	tw

-in

___ing

___ing

___ing

___ing

___ing

___ing

___ing

___ing

___ing

___ing

___ing

___ing

n	fl	r	th
cr	k	str	w
f	d	s	wr
j	spr	sw	z

-ing

Name: _____   Date: _____

___ink   ___ink

___ink   ___ink

___ink

___ink   ___ink

___ink   ___ink

___ink   ___ink

___ink

b   m   p   st

g   cl   r   w

bl   n   shr   y

l   dr   s   th

-ink

Name: _____ Date: _____

ch	gr	r	str
b	j	sn	v
fl	sh	t	wh
d	sk	th	z

-ip

Name: _____ Date: _____

g	b	spl	s
gr	h	m	st
f	sk	p	w
qu	l	r	kn

-it

Name: _____ Date: _____

____ob ____ob

____ob ____ob ____ob

____ob ____ob ____ob

____ob ____ob ____ob

cr   j   sl   s

c   gl   p   thr

bl   l   kn   t

d   m   r   sn

-ob

Name: _____ Date: _____

___ock   ___ock

___ock   ___ock   ___ock

___ock   ___ock   ___ock

___ock   ___ock

___ock   ___ock

bl	l	fr	s
d	m	p	st
cr	n	sh	v
k	fl	r	kn

-ock

Name: _____ Date: _____

Word Family
-og

____og

____og

____og

____og

____og

____og

____og

____og

____og

____og

____og

____og

b	fr	j	sm
cl	d	l	r
c	f	sl	v
fl	h	m	th

-og

Name: _____   Date: _____

___op   ___op

___op

___op

___op

___op

___op

___op

___op

___op

___op

___op

ch   h   pl   t
c   dr   n   sh
cr   m   pr   v
d   fl   p   tr

-op

Name: _____ Date: _____

b   sh   j   p

bl   f   sp   r

c   g   n   kn

gr   h   tr   s

-ot

Name: _____   Date: _____

c	h	shr	t
cl	j	r	tr
f	scr	s	st
gr	n	sn	wh

-ub

___uck

___uck

___uck

___uck

___uck

___uck

___uck

___uck

___uck

___uck

___uck

___uck

b	g	m	tr
cl	st	n	r
d	j	str	s
pl	l	p	t

-uck

Name: _____ Date: _____

____ug   ____ug

____ug   ____ug

____ug

____ug   ____ug

____ug

____ug   ____ug

____ug

shr	g	pl	s
c	b	m	sn
d	h	r	t
ch	j	sm	wh

-ug

Word Family Trees © 2011 by Scholastic Teaching Resources, page 34

Name: _____ Date: _____

__ump

__ump

__ump

__ump

__ump

__ump

__ump

__ump

__ump

__ump

__ump

__ump

cl   d   sh   p

b   pl   l   th

c   h   n   y

gr   j   st   tr

-ump

Name: _____ Date: _____

ch   h   m   fl
b   shr   r   w
d   j   sk   sp
dr   k   s   tr

-unk

Name: _____ Date: _____

___ail

___ail

___ail

___ail

___ail

___ail

___ail

___ail

___ail

___ail

___ail

___ail

b	qu	m	t
d	j	shr	w
ch	fl	p	sn
f	k	s	tr

-ail

Name: _____ Date: _____

_____ain   _____ain

_____ain   _____ain   _____ain

_____ain   _____ain   _____ain

_____ain   _____ain   _____ain

_____ain

wh	h	pl	t
d	dr	p	st
ch	m	spr	v
g	gr	r	br

-ain

Name: _____ Date: _____

___ake
___ake
___ake
___ake
___ake
___ake
___ake
___ake
___ake
___ake
___ake
___ake
___ake

b	m	r	sn
br	n	qu	v
c	gr	s	st
fl	p	sh	w

-ake

Name: _____ Date: _____

___ale ___ale

___ale ___ale

___ale

___ale ___ale

___ale

___ale ___ale

___ale

___ale

sh	l	gl	t
b	cr	p	st
g	m	ch	v
h	sc	s	wh

-ale

Name: _____ Date: _____

__ame

__ame

__ame

__ame

__ame

__ame

__ame

__ame

__ame

__ame

__ame

b	f	l	p
bl	g	fl	s
c	gr	n	sh
d	j	fr	t

-ame

Name: _____ Date: _____

___ate ___ate
___ate ___ate ___ate
___ate ___ate
___ate ___ate
___ate ___ate ___ate

cr	g	sk	r
d	qu	l	st
gr	h	sn	v
f	pl	m	sh

-ate

Name: _____ Date: _____

Word Family
-ay

_____ay
_____ay
_____ay
_____ay
_____ay
_____ay
_____ay
_____ay
_____ay
_____ay
_____ay
_____ay

w	gr	j	st
ch	z	spr	b
d	pl	l	v
bl	h	m	tr

-ay

Word Family Trees © 2011 by Scholastic Teaching Resources, page 43

Name: _____ Date: _____

___eat

___eat

___eat

___eat

___eat

___eat

___eat

___eat

___eat

___eat

___eat

___eat

b	ch	m	wh
bl	h	pl	p
d	cl	n	r
g	j	tr	s

-eat

Name: _____   Date: _____

Word Family
-ee

b   fr   r   kn
cr   f   spr t
d   gl   s   w
fl   k   tr   thr

-ee

Word Family Trees © 2011 by Scholastic Teaching Resources, page 45

Name: _____ Date: _____

__eed

__eed

__eed

__eed

__eed

__eed

__eed

__eed

__eed

__eed

__eed

__eed

bl	g	sk	w
d	gr	r	tw
fr	h	sp	z
f	n	s	th

-eed

Word Family Trees © 2011 by Scholastic Teaching Resources, page 46

Name: _____ Date: _____

___eep

___eep

___eep

___eep

___eep

___eep

___eep

___eep

___eep

___eep

___eep

___eep

___eep

b	qu	k	tw
ch	f	sl	v
d	sh	p	w
cr	j	sw	st

-eep

Name: _____ Date: _____

___ice

___ice

___ice

___ice

___ice

___ice

___ice

___ice

___ice

___ice

___ice

d	pr	m	r
ch	k	sp	t
g	sl	n	thr
fl	l	tw	v

-ice

Name: _____ Date: _____

br   gl   pr   t
d   l   sl   str
ch   qu   s   w
h   r   sn   tw

-ide

Name: _____ Date: _____

d   l   fl   s

br   m   p   kn

f   fr   r   t

g   n   pl   v

-ight

Name: _____ Date: _____

__ine

__ine

__ine

__ine

__ine

__ine

__ine

__ine

__ine

__ine

__ine

__ine

cr   j   sp   v

d   shr   m   sw

sh   k   n   z

f   l   p   wh

-ine

Name: _____ Date: _____

___y   ___y

___y   ___y   ___y

___y   ___y   ___y

___y   ___y

___y   ___y

m	fl	bl	tr
cr	fr	sh	k
b	pr	sk	tw
dr	j	sp	wh

-y

Word Family Trees © 2011 by Scholastic Teaching Resources, page 52

Name: _____ Date: _____

br   j   sp   r
c   gl   n   w
ch   l   st   y
g   sm   p   str

-oke

Name: _____ Date: _____

___one

___one

___one

___one

___one

___one

___one

___one

___one

___one

___one

cl	h	pr	w
b	ph	s	st
dr	l	sh	z
c	p	t	tw

-one

Name: _____ Date: _____

___ow

___ow

___ow

___ow

___ow

___ow

___ow

___ow

___ow

___ow

___ow

___ow

b	gr	l	sn
bl	j	sh	t
d	qu	m	cr
gl	k	r	kn

-ow

Name: _____ Date: _____

l g sc s

sm h m t

c squ n w

f b r st

-all

Name: _____ Date: _____

_____ar

_____ar

_____ar

_____ar

_____ar

_____ar

_____ar

_____ar

_____ar

_____ar

b	bl	n	st
ch	j	sp	v
c	m	p	z
f	sc	t	th

-ar

Name: _____   Date: _____

_____are

_____are

_____are

_____are

_____are

_____are

_____are

_____are

_____are

_____are

_____are

_____are

cr	d	squ	s
b	pl	g	w
gl	f	st	sp
c	sh	r	m

-are

Name: _____ Date: _____

b	gr	m	st
Cl	h	sp	v
d	l	s	y
j	sh	p	wh

-ark

Name: _____ Date: _____

___aw

___aw

___aw

___aw

___aw

___aw

___aw

___aw

___aw

___aw

___aw

___aw

cl	l	str	t
c	fl	r	th
dr	p	sl	y
j	pr	s	tr

-aw

Name: _____ Date: _____

___ore

___ore

___ore

___ore

___ore

___ore

___ore

___ore

___ore

___ore

___ore

___ore

b	fr	p	st
bl	m	sh	t
c	sc	s	th
ch	n	sn	w

-ore

Word Family Trees © 2011 by Scholastic Teaching Resources, page 61

Name: _____ Date: _____

__oop

__oop

__oop

__oop

__oop

__oop

__oop

__oop

__oop

b	sc	l	sw
c	h	sn	r
dr	j	st	t
f	sl	m	tr

-oop

Name: _____ Date: _____

___out ___out

___out ___out ___out

___out ___out ___out

___out ___out ___out

b   cl   k   tr

sc   g   sp   p

sh   h   st   r

f   sn   n   spr

-out

Name: _____   Date: _____

Word Family

_____